Getting Organised

Laying Lasting Foundations with Love

Angela Ruby

CONTENTS

In loving memory of my beloved Mother:

Rubeina Richardson

Nyame Nti

By the Grace of the Almighty

ABOUT THE AUTHOR

Angela Ruby has an Honours degree in education. She has over 20 years' experience in teaching primary and adult education and has gone on to develop and deliver a wide range of community based learning programmes. She is the founder of *A Call to Love*, a Black Women's self-empowerment course first delivered in 2002.

She has a professional interest in issues of governance, has served on a number of community forums and school governing bodies and was Chair of Governors at her children's primary school.

With extensive experience working within her local community, Angela led a two-year campaign to set up London's very first parish council, the Queen's Park Community Council (QPCC), and was the founding chair of the QPCC for the first two years when it was legislated into life in 2014.

In 2015, she was recognised with a PowerSis Award for her outstanding political activism.

Angela Ruby is available for presentations and facilitating workshops on 'Getting Organised' and can be contacted via: *www.angelaruby.com*

INTRODUCTION

An array of ills continues to pervade the black community here in the UK. People of the African Diaspora living here and throughout Europe, feature disproportionately in many statistics documenting a range of persistent educational, health, social and economic disadvantages and challenges. There is much to be addressed ranging from an upsurge in youth violence, the much talked about 'school to prison pipeline' that begins with schools and a growing number of nurseries side-lining and excluding pupils of African Caribbean descent from an early age, to the less spoken about domestic abuse, child abuse and mental health issues.

A determined effort has to be made to build on many of the successful initiatives set up specifically to tackle such issues and any effort to organise collectively must be harnessed in a manner that has a positive impact and effects lasting change. The days of soldiering along alone are ineffective and outdated. A systematic sustenance of mainstream dogma that places the black community at the bottom of the pile due to the prevalence of a white supremacist doctrine, otherwise referred to as 'racism' has to be attacked and challenged with a strategic, long sighted and sustainable approach.

Getting Organised, Laying Lasting Foundations with Love is designed to provide a straightforward resource for different groups and organisations, working primarily within the black community, who are interested in building and demonstrating their capacity to deliver services and projects that address the imbalance and is intended to capitalise on the common interest of those who are an active part of any forward-thinking group or organisation. It is not advocating separatism, rather it is acknowledging of a specific malaise attributable to a specific demographic and it accepts that there are other groups subject to systematic failures.

If it is mutually beneficial to work with people who are not of African heritage, it should be accepted that a strong sense of identity and outcomes are prerequisites for any collaboration to minimise dilution of the primary purpose of efforts to advance the specific plight of black people here in the UK.

The guide acknowledges that different groups will have different aims and objectives and the methodology that is presented can be used by any group to support a more effective way of achieving their goals and working together towards a common set of outcomes. It will prove most helpful for those groups who are at the early stages of formation and can also serve as a useful reference point for strengthening management and user involvement in existing established groups.

It further seeks to reinforce the notion that varied community groups and projects can co-exist peacefully alongside each other and most importantly that such individual groups, projects and organisations find a way to connect and work together with purpose that is beneficial to all concerned.

An underlying belief in writing this guide is that in any endeavour to strive towards a more widely accepted shared purpose, no one community effort should be considered more or less important or of more or less value than another. It accepts that each individual group can bring something of value to the table and further accepts that there are many paths to take when climbing a mountain.

If working more effectively together, as a people, can serve to increase the chances of achieving a common end goal, one of greater cohesion and unity, with improved social, economic and general life conditions within the black community, then acknowledging differences in processes, each of which has a distinct role to play for the greater good, must be accepted so that goal is not compromised.

The nurturing thread running throughout the suggested steps is aimed solely and simply at supporting those people and groups within the black community who want to work towards a common sense of unity. So in this endeavour, the premise is **that the black community is in need of increased cohesion, strategic planning and direction to overcome many issues**.

This guide is presented in two parts.

Part 1 – The Why?

Part 1 provides an overview of some of the reasons that led me to producing this guide. It explores the idea of community in relation to the black community and presents an overview of the status quo – *the why*.

Part 2 – The How?

2A: Part 2 takes you through a series of steps designed to guide you through setting up a group or strengthening an existing one – *the how*.

2B: It also outlines the Loving Principles and the need to inject love into any community effort to establish, maintain and sustain collective works.

Part 1. Why?

The time is always right to do what is right

Martin Luther King

WHAT IS COMMUNITY?

The word community is derived from the Latin *communitas*, meaning public spirit, fellowship or common unity. It generally describes a group of people that share a common interest, location or ownership and is commonly referred to as having a sense of 'common unity'. These days, with the onslaught of social networking, there exists a number of virtual communities where people are in contact with others who may or may not share any common interests or locality.

Has this added to the troublesome task of defining one's community?

Most people will accept that they belong to more than one community and these different communities can range, for example, from where a person lives, works and spends their leisure time to which social network sites they frequent, what books they read and which religion they belong to.

CAN YOU DEFINE YOUR COMMUNITY?

Back in the day, defining our community – our local area – was clear-cut. As children, we were more likely to go to schools within our localities, frequent local play centres and youth clubs and we were more likely to shop on the local high street with our parents. As such, we tended to see more of the same people – people who also lived in our neighbourhood. There is a much-quoted scenario where, if as a child, you were spotted by an elder in the local area in a compromising position, word of any wrongdoing would reach your home before you did. No mobile phones existed, yet the people grapevine was strong; it meant that people spoke to each other and they knew each other, often by name. But communities have changed according to the times we live in and the way people do things has changed along with that.

Nowadays, many parents want their children to go to the 'best' school even if it means a two-hour journey each way. They also fear their children being outside the home, on the street – so playing outside is a no-no and any extracurricular activities likely involve a taxi service there and back. There is no time to meet and greet any of the neighbours, who are actually in their own cars doing the same thing, so there are very few people to pass on the street even if you do decide to walk. So the citing of changing times remains troublesome when it is in fact changing people and their habits that continue to drive changing times.

We all live somewhere. We need to take ownership of our local areas and minimise the outsourcing of our needs to other areas. Our children need a safe and friendly environment in which to grow up and flourish, and fleeing from the areas in which we live surely cannot be a solution. With this in mind, I believe that one of the primary communities to which you belong is often the neighbourhood in which you live.

IT TAKES A WHOLE COMMUNITY...

In support of this stance, on the progressive black community circuit there is a much-quoted African proverb – "it takes a whole village to raise a child". It refers to and reinforces the need for local neighbourhoods to be more self-sufficient and to serve as a starting point for change or a necessary return to a time when we interacted more with people we live in close proximity to. The safe raising of our children comes with a greater challenge when this often-quoted village is 'virtual' and in no way resembles a physical space.

As testimony to the fact that people will and do form links with those they are in close proximity to, very few children are without friends that they met via school and most adults go on to form close relationships with the people they work with. These community bonds at work, at school and wherever else people meet others on a regular basis, are attractive mainly because having and feeling a sense of belonging is a very real and basic human need. This is not to say that we do away with such bonds, rather we need to examine if such bonds are useful extras: supplements to our sense of community or substitutes because in these current times, we are without the village, the local community in which we live.

The closest some of us from the African Diaspora came to that village was arguably as children of the 1960s – 1980s when we lived in clusters in parts of London and other inner cities prior to the introduction of the 'right to buy' era, when many were encouraged to buy and sell their homes for profit. This led to the displacement of our collective presence in certain areas and any reappearance of black people in certain areas is as a result of 'newer' arrivals to the UK. In the absence of an existing strong black infrastructure on which to build in certain areas, the floundering continues and many feel we are back to where we started over 50 years ago. If we did, in the past, try to replicate the village through pardner, sou sou, (a collective means to saving and amassing funds), and house parties, that village has long been lost.

In this modern digital era, many of us are opting for shared online interests; significant numbers of us are members of a large number of groups and we continue to connect as long as the information being fed to us is of some benefit. I myself am a member of a number of online forums, groups and networks – the labels are endless. This begs the question 'amongst all of this, exactly what is being touted as the village'? Is the reference to the proverb wishful thinking? How far are we prepared to go in our efforts to re-establish the much quoted village – or is this just talk?

MORE IMPORTANT FOR SOME...

For many of us of African heritage, we have a sense of belonging which transcends the house we pay council tax on and the area around it. Many people from the African Diaspora have a strong affiliation with the black community. At first sight, this term appears straightforward enough, however, the so-called black community is arguably far from one large, homogenous group that envelopes all black people living here in the UK.

About 10 years ago, I carried out a small-scale piece of online research and asked over 200 black women living mainly in the UK to provide an apt label to describe their heritage, their ethnic origin. The answer to that one question yielded 96 different responses and the multitude of labels used ranged from the simple 'Black British', 'West Indian' and 'Black Caribbean' or 'Black African' to the more convoluted 'Black African Caribbean' and 'Black British Caribbean' descent! Having recently conducted a sample check, I am fairly confident that not a great deal has changed in this time and these stats continue to reflect this gulf in a common named identity.

Whilst the sheer number of different responses was unsettling, of no surprise was the fact that there would be *different* responses. We don't all see or indeed refer to ourselves in the same way and there are a number of reasons for this. This toolkit cannot do Justice to the complex and lengthy reasons for these varied ethnic perceptions. However, I think it is important for us to linger here a while because often when we look to discuss the many challenges facing people from the African Diaspora living here in the UK, we look to the USA for some of the possible solutions.

Many, though not all, black people living in the USA refer to themselves as African American. We here in the UK appear not to have as commonly accepted a collective identity label. Rather our links with the various Caribbean Islands serve to reinforce the separation and many of us cling tightly to the differences between the islands, serving to render us further disconnected from each other. Ownership of any ethnic label that includes the term 'African' presents challenges and is troublesome because many black people here in the UK continue to find it hard to use the term in favour of the islands of their parents or grandparents. I call it the *too many ancestors away for it to have a part to play* syndrome. This is a crying shame.

Moving forward, for the purpose of this text it is useful to present my broadest definition of the term 'black community' which is defined here as people of the African Diaspora living in the UK. I will continue to use and make reference to the term *black community* and any differentiation of the meaning will be linked to the individual reading this text.

THE BLACK COMMUNITY – OUR CHALLENGES?

Before taking you through the suggested steps towards strengthening our community, I would like to briefly present some of the reasons behind why I decided to produce this guide and why I think it is important.

A couple of years ago, I attended a workshop on male-female relationships within the black community. Part of the presentation included a film clip of an old musical. The theme of the clip was *tradition*, which included a male narrator who was singing about the different roles and responsibilities of each member of the small village. He made reference to the different tasks carried out by the men, women, boys and girls. When questioned why this is so, he sang loud and proud "tradition!"

On being probed further, he was unable to identify the source of this tradition, instead asserting 'it's just the way things have always been done'. People of African heritage who have found themselves in Europe mainly via the Caribbean have lost a common sense of their traditions. That is not to say that there exists no tradition; rather the question is whose tradition has been adopted and where has it come from? Like the man in the film clip, it is hard to ascertain exactly when something has been started if it is seemingly something that has always been done. The current and continuing plight of many black people living in the UK is in stark contrast to a culture that historically was steeped in tradition.

The current movement of black advancement encompasses a plethora of doctrine. Some advocate a return to African spirituality that includes meditation, vegan and raw food choices and African yoga; others encourage a withdrawal from the use of TV and the wider media. A widely-accepted compass for a way forward is one that views economic growth, black history and knowledge of cultural identity as some of the most important cornerstones in reclaiming our heritage.

BLACK ECONOMICS

Many participants of progressive black movements insist upon a solution steeped in economic intelligence and growth. Yes, I agree, and in many ways, this is why organisation is essential. We as a community are noted for being active consumers. It is further purported that our collective spending power, being quite considerable, could have a significant impact on furthering a multitude of community efforts with economic investment and growth at the heart of our spending, if channelled in the right direction.

As I write the final pages of this guide, we have witnessed a general election, a number of terrible incidents resulting in the loss of human life that have included explosions and even more tragically a firing inferno that is unprecedented in modern Britain in 2017. All of these tragedies have ignited deep human concern and a rallying of personal and collective efforts to contribute both materially and financially to the huge losses experienced by survivors of these tragedies and in respect of the families and friends who lost loved ones.

Social media, having provided an outlet for armchair journalism, was awash with comments comparing the crowdfunding efforts of these tragedies to the crowdfunding efforts of many cash-strapped black organisations. Not wishing to compare the two in the light of such human tragedy, it is apparent that the nature of human behaviour is one that, sadly, is at times more reactive than proactive and it is without doubt that loss of life trumps most other instances of suffering. I am also of the opinion that the large amounts of money raised are not purely from the black community. Appeals such as these have a more mainstream presence and tend to garner interest from a cross section of the nation.

All that said, a glaringly obvious thing to note is that many organisations that appeal for public donations must recognise the need for accountability. For example, I was recently sent an appeal for donations towards a community venture and was concerned to note that the means by which to donate was given as a personal bank account. Along with the appeal was a footnote chastising the black community for their lack of support. This has to stop and stop now. We know that we have a more recent history of collective economic lack and we certainly accept that there is much healing to be done. Thus, we need to allay some of the fears on both sides by eliminating the lowest common denominator of mistrust by setting ourselves up in a way that fosters and encourages financial giving and support without suspicion.

Furthermore, we need to consider if we are unwittingly calling on the same group of people for support, financially or otherwise. Are certain projects 'palatable' enough to appeal to larger numbers of people? Have specific interest groups been targeted for their support? Do they even know your group exists? What is clear is that we cannot continue with an over reliance on a very small section of the black community to ensure our success. This is why we need to get organised, stay organised and widen participation once we have a proven track record for achieving results that directly impact on improving black people's lives and addressing some of the aforementioned challenges.

I cannot complete this section without briefly acknowledging an ongoing point of disagreement in regards to funding. This continues to be an area that centres on the distinction between being funded or self-funded and I'm not sure that this ought to be one of the key issues in the scope of the work that needs to be done. Great if you are in a position to self-fund and great again if you're able to attract external funding for your project. Of course, there is the possibility that some groups seeking external funds may well adapt their outcomes to suit the funder, or indeed tailor their projects to 'fit'. Equally, there are the self-funded who may have to limit their outcomes and/ or tailor their aims in line with their budgets. The decision as to how a group secures the financial means to execute their work is a decision for the management arm of that organisation.

The bigger issue I believe is sustainability and accountability. These are very often key questions posed on most applications for funding and addressing this is fundamental to the longevity of the group, whichever funding route is taken.

Self-funding, whilst providing greater autonomy, should not mean a lack of clear accounting processes are not adhered to and accountability for funded projects should go beyond satisfying the funders.

Stories of poor financial practices need to be balanced by highlighting those groups and organisations that operate good practice, with sound financial principles, be it funded or self-funded, we need to increase their existence.

IS BLACK HISTORY THE ANSWER?

There is a high number of initiatives, projects and programmes abound that are aimed at positivity and development within the black community. Many advocate the need for knowledge of the self and for this the prerequisite is knowing one's history. Another well-known quote is that of the great and inspired Marcus Mosiah Garvey, who is reported to have stated, "A people without knowledge of their history are like a tree without roots". The leaders in this field range from those who come out in full force during Black History months and those who are ever-present all year round.

History is an interesting subject, and some knowledge of one's history is crucial for many reasons; it gives us some insight into how things have gone before us. In this way we are able to make sense of things in the present and those yet to come: to discern a proper path for the future.

History is something that embeds itself within the human psyche over time. It literally gets recorded in our DNA. But we are a long way from the intuitive beings we once were.

For many of us from the black community living here in the UK, the snippets of British and world history we are familiar with have been more or less fed to us over many years, beginning in our infancy, from mainstream books and anecdotes. But written knowledge today plays as much, or more of a role, in informing us of our past and we must dig deeply into this vein because written history is sometimes skewed.

Rarely will an ordinary layperson receive a piece of antiquated information without seeking it out. Getting into the necessary mind-set that one will consciously seek out the truth about one's past, whether as an individual or as a group, or at the very least discover the path that got them where they are today, and taking into consideration their personal ability or inclination to remember or document this information for others, takes a great deal of will, discipline and dedication. Unfortunately, we are not all willing to be historians.

Much of Africa's contributions to the world have been lost, erased or destroyed and attempting to reverse this loss is a huge challenge. In no way am I suggesting that we do not rise to this challenge. February and October present a wealth of cramming opportunities. Many scholars deliver a sustained stream of black history topics for the history hungry to feast upon. I am simply curious to know how many of us of the first generation, those who are responsible for running with the baton, are able to retain this information and weave it into our fading memory banks.

Consider a European figure such as Napoleon; we all know this name and some of us may even be able to quote some of his exploits of centuries past. My guess is that few of us would have gleaned this information from a one-off lecture. Tales of 'prominent' figures in the one-dimensional history of Europe are embedded within the European culture: during school history lessons, on the TV, stage and radio, in tongue in cheek advertisements and jokes, in town centres, street names, at bus stops and pubs. Embedded! The same can be said for royal figureheads such as Queen Victoria and the Prince of Wales; I think we all might have a pub in our local area bearing one of these names.

In the Caribbean, history lessons often reinforced that one dimensional European world view. This is not to say none of our distinct and great history was taught to us, only that our ancestral history was not reinforced and embedded within the culture. Our parents and grandparents were ill equipped to teach us any history about African influences around the world or about the European culture from a black perspective.

And we are yet to arrive at a time when this is indeed the case. The question to ask here is *how realistic is it to expect something that does not serve the status quo of false white supremacy to become a part of the dominant culture*? A culture that places 'whiteness' at the centre of universe, with easy access to information and all things supporting that stance. How can we ensure that our people have widespread, meaningful and systematic access to this information which does not likely involve the time and commitment of preparing a thesis?

Valiant efforts to teach ourselves black history will, in my opinion, go a long way to emancipating our people, and these efforts would be best focused among the young, who have the learning capacity and time to assimilate this information into their psyches.

A lack of knowledge of our history and our traditions equates to a lack of a common culture and therefore a lack of cultural identity. This, in turn, creates a fragile foundation upon which to build a strong sense of personal identity. So, at this point in time, I think it is fair to say that we are in a place where we will continue to have differing views and opinions about the best ways to progress. Once again, though, there are many ways to climb this mountain.

RECLAIMING OUR CULTURE

Following on from the brief reference to history, I naturally have to include here a few musings about culture as that has invariably popped up in the dialogue about history. The Oxford English Dictionary defines culture as: 'the ideas, customs and social behaviour of a particular people or society' and further defines it as 'the attitude and behaviour characteristic of a particular social group'.

African civilisation was a remarkable setting for all manner of global trends including spirituality, education: mathematics and science, trade, travel, food and farming, relationships, community, raw materials, and architecture to name a few. If you want to know more, see any of renowned historian Robin Walker's brilliant books on African history.

The onslaught of the lengthy and dark period of transatlantic chattel slavery savagely and mercilessly ripped away the many cultural traditions that African people had long established. The enslaved African people were forcibly prevented from using their own names, their language, their spirituality and their clothes as they were viciously bullied and beaten into adopting a culture foreign to their own; a culture that had at its core economic and territorial gain and a sustained practice of the dehumanisation of Africans in order to justify such rampant greed.

Populations in the Caribbean that endured this atrocity developed coping mechanisms to survive and an 'island' culture was born with certain emerging traits particular to certain islands. But what of the significant numbers of children born in the UK following an invitation to their parents from 'Mother Commonwealth' to come to England to service the Transport System and the National Health Service? What we need to know is how do black people here do things, how do they know this and who has passed on this information?

As per the definition above, *culture* is simply the way a group of people with something in common does things. What is done collectively is based on the value system adopted; what is considered to be important. Groups of people round the globe are often easily identifiable by their culture based on practices over and above the colour of their skin; having black skin is not a culture.

Just for the record, many times I have been told stories about a public display of poor behaviour and just how embarrassing it was to bear witness to a brother or sister with little regard for self. Our self-perception, both individually and collectively, is steeped in negativity and has become fragile; if we feel so strongly when in the company of a badly-behaved brother or sister, we should learn to feel just as strongly in the absence of negative attention-seeking behaviours. Why wait until the presence of shame to identify with others in your self image? Owning shame only serves to add to a poor self image.

As such, every culture shares those things they deem important and practice every day, such as: Language, birth names, greetings and salutations – how elders are addressed, clothing ranging from everyday wear to occasion wear, rituals around birth, marriage and death, naming ceremonies, rites of passage, food, including how it is prepared and cooked and that which is not eaten, gender roles to include boys and girls through to adulthood, and usually some form of spirituality based on a belief system that there is a higher being. This list is far from all-inclusive, but demonstrates that who we are, how we think and what we do are most often shaped by a cultural affiliation.

One's culture is the foundation for building self-knowledge and an understanding of those who are like you. It is a woven fabric of connectedness. A people lacking in culture are gravely at risk. To put it mildly, black people living in the UK have a fragmented cultural identity with the gaps being filled by bits of culture borrowed from others. And because different people borrow different bits – the result is a fragmented group that lacks its own unique identity and has failed to preserve its culture and, even with the best will in the world remains incomplete.

This is the context for this guide:
Strengthening our communities
Why we need to get organised

It is a simple recognition of the pressing need to work towards an uplifting and more collective cultural consensus. One that recognises that different people will seek to achieve different outcomes. All that is required is a collaborative effort on the works in hand. As we march towards re-establishing a common culture that is founded in a common goal to uniting in empowering its people to enhance its economic growth and celebrate our culture and history, we do so with an acceptance that there is a lack of awareness of black cultural history among mainstream blacks as well as an economic stronghold. We will each, therefore, need to find a way up the mountain that suits our particular group, project and affiliated community.

We will need to accept that, at this moment in time, different people will map out different routes and take different journeys. The key buy-in for growth at this stage is commitment to moving within pockets of the black community on all levels with an eye toward reconnecting us with our authentic selves and an objective of taking those whose self-esteem has plummeted into darkness and self-abhorrence to their rightful place on the planet.

Part 2 a. The How?

*If you want to go fast, **go alone***
*If you want to go far, **go together***

African Proverb

DEFINING YOUR COMMUNITY

I have met a vast number of people within the black community who are soldiering on doing some great work. I am often humbled by the selflessness of those who work tirelessly for the betterment of a wider community in spite of the ad hoc service on offer.

One of the many variables relating to the inconsistency in attendance at many events, I believe, may lie in the broadness of the term 'black community' and what I call the 'fishing syndrome', which relies on casting the net far and wide in the hope of a catch.

Any business selling a product or service must first define their target market so as not to waste their message on the wrong audience. Organising a group should be done in much the same way businesses set up their structure. For this reason, I advocate, as a starting point, the need to define the section of the community you seek to reach and to cast your net to that defined demographic; that intended section of the population and community.

Arguably, some of us accept that a random black community does not exist. We continue to cater to something that is difficult to define, without using filter to hone in on the group we want to attract. Your group leaders should first define who their target audience is – who they want to reach specifically – and 'advertise' to them. In this way, with correctly defined members, the group's objective can begin to break the status quo. This is not about separation per se, but about having a clearly defined target audience to ensure that the service delivered serves as it is intended.

Some very good examples already exist and they are far too many to list here. Consider if you would like your community to serve women, for example, then hone your audience further. Do you want to target mothers only? Women of a certain age? Single women? Working women? Your audience can be defined any way you need it to be. Are you looking for men? Single fathers? Parents in general, people living in a certain locality, people with a particular interest, profession or a certain skill set? Perhaps your target is children and young people. It is a rare service that can be all things to all people, so it's vital to the group's objective message to clearly, specifically and intentionally define who that message is meant for.

As stated previously, a person often views themselves as belonging to more than one community. You will be hard pressed to identify a place that you can go to that addresses all of your needs. In defining your community, some of you, I hope, will recognise the importance and power of locality in having the potential to address some key issues endemic within that elusive 'black community'. Ask yourself if you want the service you offer to be additional to everyday lives or an integral part of it?

DEFINING YOUR COMMUNITY – ACTIVITY/KEY POINTS:

Who are you trying to reach?

_____

_____

_____

_____

_____

How have you identified your target group?

_____

_____

_____

_____

Do any other groups exist to serve this target audience? (may be useful to define a geographical area)

_____

_____

_____

_____

_____

Comments:

_____

_____

_____

_____

DECIDING ON A STRUCTURE

To help with deciding on the best structure for your group or organisation it is worth bearing in mind the following:

I.   **Purpose** – what is the primary purpose of your group? What are you setting out to achieve?

II. **Powers** – what legal requirements are necessary to achieve your purpose?

III. **People** – who will be responsible for the purpose and powers of the group: management committee, trustees?

I. YOUR PURPOSE: WHAT ARE YOU TRYING TO ACHIEVE?

This begins with your mission statement. It should consist of a few lines that clearly state the goals and objectives of your group. You will also need a plan. It is one thing to know what you would like to accomplish, but you also need to know how you are going to get there. What steps will the group take to achieve those aims? This statement should be something that is reached in consultation with others with an active interest in what you hope to achieve. In other words, the group leaders should work to hone in on the mission of the group and put it in writing.

Good practice suggests that any mission statement should be formed after a period of consultation among key stakeholders of the service. Potential objectives should be presented, hashed out and finally decided upon. However, in order to define objectives, research will be necessary to uncover exactly what services are needed. Defining a target audience is part of this. How else will you ensure that the service your group aims to provide is a service that is needed or even wanted by them? Some organisations persist in providing services for which there is little appetite or interest.

I have equally witnessed a great many well-attended events with a hungry audience that is at times left wanting. This mismatch in the service (event) and the user (audience) can be avoided by ensuring that what you deliver is what people want. There should also be clarity regarding any necessary follow up or ongoing user involvement. Any follow up will also help to widen participation in your group's activities.

Once your objectives are defined, you will begin planning how to go about implementing your service and attracting your audience. This aspect of planning can borrow from the many sound principles of effective marketing. Something I have come across repeatedly is the elevator pitch. This is a tactic used by sales people, actors, and anyone who needs to 'sell' a product or service. You must be able to clearly and succinctly state your mission, purpose, product, or whatever you're offering in 30 seconds. The idea is that if you are clear about what your group seeks to do and are able to communicate this with clarity in 30 seconds, you will keep the attention of the listener, and you will be on your way to making your group's vision a reality.

Have you ever witnessed the building of a new housing complex or shopping arena? In days of old, this type of site would be in full glare of all passers-by, though nowadays there is a likely to be some kind of shield, often complete with the name of the contractors and possibly some fancy artist's impression of the final product. The point to bear in mind is that whilst the new site remains out of site and under construction, you can bet your bottom dollar that the laying of the foundation is likely to be a pretty messy endeavour. For one, there is preparation of the groundwork and in the event of uncovering major issues during excavation, this all adds to the apparent mess.

Setting up a group can be likened to a building under construction. The foundation needs to be strong in order to support the structure. And this section is all about getting the underlying strengths in place.

There are a number of different structures that can be adopted and the one you choose depends on what you want to achieve. Thus, you would need to have had addressed your aims and objectives in order to progress onto this next step. The essential thing to remember is that the foundation you are looking to lay will determine how your group will be governed – your governance – and this can take many forms.

SOME IMPORTANT THINGS TO CONSIDER...

I. **Create a Mission Statement**: Whether you decide on a business structure or a more charitable enterprise, your Mission Statement states exactly why your organisation exists, its goals and objectives and the difference you seek to make. It should be clearly and concisely written. This statement can also convey your uniqueness; it should distinguish your group from others of the same or similar type.

II. **Create a Plan**: Your plan should be a strategic framework that not only sets out a clear vision for the future of the organisation, but also demonstrates the strength of the management behind the organisation. This is your Road Map. Be specific. Use timelines. What do you want to accomplish within a certain time frame? Consider costs. Where and how will you get any necessary funding? Who will perform certain tasks within the plan? What is your secondary plan if you come across any snags in meeting the plan's timeline? Define priorities; what needs to be done first in order for the rest of the plan to work? Being flexible is important. If something doesn't work, don't give up and assume the entire plan is wrong. Reassess it and make necessary changes so that you can continue along.

III. **Implement your Plan**: A good organisational plan provides direction to everyone involved in the initial organisation of the group. Such coherence provides consistency and gives a point of reference when things aren't panning out as expected. And this may happen more than once, so it's important to be flexible and creative. Your mission statement will remain the same, but how you achieve it may change as the plan evolves.

YOUR MISSION/PURPOSE: WHY DOES YOUR GROUP EXIST?
ACTIVITY/KEY POINTS:

What is the purpose of your group's existence?

_____

_____

_____

_____

What are you seeking to achieve?

_____

_____

_____

_____

Is there a clearly identified need for your existence?

_____

_____

_____

_____

_____

How do you know this?

_____

_____

_____

_____

Comments:

_____

_____

_____

ORGANISATIONAL PLAN – A STRATEGIC FRAMEWORK:
WHAT TO INCLUDE:

1. **Mission statement**: the no waffle 'why' your organisation exists.

2. **Purpose**: Aims & Objectives are the key activities your organisation intends to deliver – these cover the strategy/aims that relate to the what and the how of your work (which considers the how/what/where/when/cost etc).

3. **Background**: Take an overview and review your past work. Refer to your track record (if you have one) and past achievements. This will allow you to gauge what has worked for you in the past and what hasn't worked. View it in the context of your new organisation's mission statement and plan.

4. **Priorities**: Determine which of the necessary tasks in your plan should be done first in order for the rest to be implemented. For example, you can't send out flyers without funding or defining demographics. Arrange the necessary tasks clearly within your set timelines. Make sure everyone involved knows that their task relies on the prioritised task, and vice versa. This will provide context for the founding group leaders. They will know what is needed and when for your organisation to move forward.

5. **Strengths and weaknesses**: Identify the qualifications and strong points of group leaders. People work best when they are better suited to one particular task over another. Determine any training needs and find resources to help in that area. In this way, your group's plan will have the ability to effectively deliver.

6. **Finances**: Good financial management is crucial to fulfilling the group's goals, so you will need to create a Financial Plan as well. How, exactly, is money to be spent? Be specific. This is separate to any financial regulations required by law. It is your Financial Statement or Financial Report. It will document all the financial activities of the group and should include any assets the group has such as property, buildings, lease or rental income, cash inputs, donations, and so on.

7. **Strategies for development**: Set targets and objectives to develop the organisation further.

8. **Monitoring and evaluation**: How will you know if you are achieving what you set out to do? Do build in outcomes for the group's aims. How will this be measured? What determines when a task is completed or when an objective is achieved? Will it be defined as a certain number of members, a specific financial amount, particular public events taking place, testing or demonstration of members' growth? How exactly will the group's growth be defined? These things should be monitored and periodically evaluated.

9. **Timeline**: This can be a simple 'at a glance' tool to note what will get done, when and by whom.

10. **Review**: This is important in any plan. There should be an approximate date given for reviewing the plan to see what's working and what's not. Your plan should not be set in stone. It should be viewed as an evolving tool to be used for the ongoing journey.

Other useful info to include:

1. You may want to include any evidence of consultation with stakeholders: staff, volunteers, service users, existing funders/client organisations, other local groups

2. Can also include financial reports, insurance docs, and policies such as safeguarding, health & safety, etc.

II. YOUR POWERS

Identifying exactly what you want to achieve is the key to making any decision on how this will be achieved; how you intend to operate. You will need to identify your operational form if you're setting up an organisation, business or group aimed at helping people and/or strengthening community. For many volunteer groups working on behalf of the community, their purpose generally falls within a social remit. This may or may not be coupled with charitable aims. The most common structures for many community building and strengthening initiatives include either an:

- Unincorporated Association (Group) or
- Incorporated Organisations – Companies, Social Enterprises, Charitable Incorporated Organisations (CIOs) and Community Interest Companies (CICs)

If you want to set up a strictly profit-making enterprise, the best option is to set up as:

- Limited Liability Company
- Sole Trader
- Business Partnership

If you want to set up a venture that has social, charitable or community-based objectives, some of the best options include:

- Limited Company
- Charitable Incorporated Organisation (CIO)
- Community Interest Company (CIC)
- Charity

If you're setting up a small organisation, such as a small voluntary group or sports or member's club and don't plan to make a profit, you can operate as an Unincorporated Association instead of setting up and registering a more formal structure.

UNINCORPORATED ASSOCIATION

An unincorporated group or organisation is usually a preferred option when a number of individuals agree to come together for a common purpose generally of a social nature.

- Unincorporated associations cost nothing to set up and are relatively easy to run with their own rules set out within some kind of agreed constitution, or without.

- An unincorporated association is generally managed by a small, specific group of people known as a management committee or a management board.

- Such groups are not required to register in the UK or to be regulated by any outside bodies such as Companies House, the Charity Commission or the Financial Services Authority. This allows greater freedom than a registered company and there is no requirement to submit annual accounts.

- Unincorporated associations are free to trade and carry out general business or commercial activities

A number of groups start off this way as it allows them to 'test the water' prior to incurring any additional costs for the set-up process and beginning any formal paper trail. There is an element of risk involved with existing as an unincorporated association as such a group does not exist as a **separate legal identity**. This is an important point to consider as any contracts entered into will be done by individuals who will carry the risk of personal liability, known as unlimited liability. They may run the risk of losing their house, car or any other personal possessions of value.

Thus, such a structure should be viewed as an interim measure to adopting a more sustainable form of governance. This is certainly true if the group's longer-term vision includes becoming an employer, raising capital and entering into larger contracts including asset transfers, leases and property acquisition – all of which need to be done via a registered organisation or company.

I have included the unincorporated group as some people may wish to adopt a less formal structure, however, this should not be a reason for your group to remain without a simple system of clearly agreed operating practices. Having a constitution in place will clarify what your group has set out to achieve, how it plans to achieve this and should name the people who are responsible for leading on these terms of reference. It is an important document that communicates to your members, followers and supporters the manner in which you intend to operate.

Of note is the fact that if you intend to open a bank account in the group's name, a basic requirement is a Governing Document: a constitution, a management committee of at least three individuals and two unrelated signatories.

Also, important to note here is the fact that a number of community initiatives operating as unincorporated associations, i.e. without any formal charity or company registration, are setting up 'crowdfunding' pages as a means to raise funds for their work. This is ok. What might not prove ok or indeed sustainable in the long term is an absence of any procedures in place for accountability to those who provide the funds. Without having to adhere to any accounting regulations – to file any accounts or annual reports – it is likely that this trend will lose momentum. Good practice dictates that something should be in place to report and account for all monies received and how that money was or will be spent. This ensures continued support and transparency to satisfy both the funded and the funders (*see p 16, Black Economics*).

INCORPORATED ORGANISATION

A corporation, being a legal entity, is effectively recognized as having the same rights and privileges under the law as an individual person. As such:

- Your incorporated organisation is a corporate body with a separate legal identity from the individuals who make up the group.
- It has powers, for example, to employ people and hold property with members having limited liability in the event of the organisation going bust.
- The corporation may be run as a business or a non-profit organization.

There are four main types of company:
- Private company limited by shares
- Private company limited by guarantee
- Private unlimited company
- Public limited company

In order for your group or organisation to operate as a limited company (as one of the above), it must be registered: incorporated at Companies House under the Companies Act 2006.

Setting up as a company means the lead people of the group – the Directors – are required to file certain documents every year such as annual accounts and an annual return. Certain changes are required by law to be reported to Companies House, such as appointment or resignation of Directors and any change in address for the registered office of the company.

With incorporated companies comes the language specific to the regulations for such entities. Whereas the term *constitution* is used for unincorporated groups, more legalities are in play now that put the organisation under regulation rules. Getting to grips with terms such as *Memorandum* and *Articles of Association* are a necessary part of setting up the structure. For more information on incorporating a new company, visit: *www.companieshouse.gov.uk*

To find out which is the best one for your group, it may be best to seek professional legal advice from a solicitor or an accountant before deciding whether an incorporated company is the best way for you to run your business, community group or organisation.

It might be worth noting that the more common forms of incorporated organisation that are favoured by voluntary organisations are:

- **Company Limited by Guarantee** which can include registration as a charity, providing the objectives of the company are charitable
- **Community Interest Company**, also known as CIC, a more recent addition
- **Charitable Incorporated Organisation**, also known as CIO

COMMUNITY INTEREST COMPANY (CIC)

A CIC is a special type of limited company which exists to benefit the community rather than private shareholders.

To set up a CIC, you need to apply to Companies House, and:

- include a *community interest statement*, explaining what your business plans to do

- create an *asset lock* – a legal promise stating that the company's assets will only be used for its social objectives, and setting limits to the money it can pay to shareholders
- get your company approved by the Community Interest Company regulator

The CIC regulator has guidance on CICs, including the forms you need to set one up. A community interest company is a limited company with the same legal separation as any other company. It is an alternative option for people who want to carry out activities that are wholly intended to be of benefit to the community. A CIC can be registered as a company only once the CIC Regulator has approved an application to form a CIC. There are also a number of monitoring and regulation hoops to satisfy Companies House that the CIC is being run in the manner for which it was intended, that is, for the benefit of the community. To find out more visit the Companies House website.

REGISTERED CHARITY

There are four main types of charity structure:
1. Charitable incorporated organisation (CIO)
2. Charitable company (limited by guarantee)
3. Unincorporated association
4. Trust

1. **The Charitable Incorporated Organisation** (CIO) is the newest legal form for a charity that has been introduced in response to feedback from the charitable sector. It is a new incorporated charity structure which is not a limited company or subject to company regulation as unlike companies, CIOs do not have to register with Companies House. Instead they will have to apply to register as a CIO with the Charity Commission. Certain CIO regulations apply, however unlike companies, CIOs will not be fined for certain administrative errors like late filing of accounts. A CIO is a company-like corporate body that has the powers to own property, employ staff and enter into other contracts in its own name, separate from the individual trustees. As members of a company limited by guarantee, trustees of a CIO have limited liability for any debts if the CIO

winds up. This limited liability means that trustees may only have to pay a fixed amount or may have no liability at all.

2. **Charitable Company (limited by guarantee)** is one of the more common forms of incorporated organisation favoured by voluntary organisations and is formed by setting up a *Company Limited by Guarantee*, which can include registration as a charity providing the objectives of the company are charitable. This structure tends to generate the largest paper trail as there will be a need to satisfy and comply with the regulations and requirements of both Companies House and the Charity Commission.

3. **Unincorporated Association** has been discussed in detail above. If your group has charitable aims, is not a CIO and has an income of less than £5000, then it is not required to register with the Charity Commission and can instead simply operate as an unincorporated association. You can apply to HM Revenue and Customs to recognise your organisation as charitable so that you can claim back tax on things like Gift Aid donations. By law, if you set up a charity, you must apply to register it with the commission if it is a charitable incorporated organisation (CIO) or its annual income is more than £5,000, unless it is a specific type of charity that doesn't have to register.

4. **Trusts** involve a transfer of assets (this could be property, shares or cash) that a 'donor' signs over or uses to create a charitable foundation. In such cases, the Trust will receive instructions that the trustees will hold the assets for others: generally, for a specific group of beneficiaries. In addition to the large, well-known charitable trusts, there are a wide range of smaller trusts created to help fund a particular good cause. An advantage of the trust structure for charitable funding is that the person setting up the trust can simply indicate how they wish the funds to be used. An example would be funds earmarked for supplementary schools whose attendees are primarily or all black, but the decision about how projects should be funded would be left to the trustees.

SOME IMPORTANT THINGS TO CONSIDER...

I. Check that being a charity won't stop you doing things you want to do.
II. Charity trustees are normally unpaid volunteers - they can only be paid where it is authorised, stated in your governance documents.

III. Charities can't usually benefit anyone connected with the charity, for example giving work to a trustee's family member or company, unless it is authorised.

IV. Charities can't have a mix of charitable and non-charitable purposes

V. Charities can't take part in certain political activities, such as campaigning for a change in government

VI. in order to achieve charitable status, the group or organisation must have a minimum of £5000 turnover per annum

VII. Charities can only have purposes the law recognises as being charitable. You will need to assess whether or not the purpose of the group is charitable in the eyes of the law.

In the eyes of UK Charity Law, "To be a charity in England and Wales, everything the organisation is set up to achieve must be charitable; your charity's 'purpose' or the reason it exists. Your charity can have more than one purpose but it can't have any purposes that aren't charitable".

There are a number of criteria to satisfy the Charity Commission in order to complete the CIO registration process, but other conditions apply. Please see: *www.charitycommission.gov.uk*

Once you have checked and confirmed your eligibility to become a Charity, you will need to register your charity with either or both the Charity Commission and Companies House depending on the structure you have selected. From the point of registration, every year you will need to provide detailed information on all of your organisation's finances and activities.

Again, here you need to choose the right structure for your group, depending on whether you need it to have a corporate structure, whether your aims are wholly charitable and whether you want to have a wider membership. Many groups whose remit is exclusively charitable for public benefit naturally progress to registration as a charitable interest organisation (CIO) via the Charity Commission.

Now that I have highlighted some of the different structures available to your group for further investigation, it is worth reinforcing just how important it is to spend some time choosing the right structure. You may have seen a number of popular

TV shows that document the journey of ordinary people who have taken on the challenge of building their own houses. There is always a project deadline and it is a rare couple who manage to bring the project to completion on target. This is something to keep in mind when laying the foundations. Sometimes, something takes as long as it takes. This is not to say that an attitude of apathy is the best, rather an approach that seeks to ensure the necessary groundwork is securely in place before any attempt to start building. Back to the building analogy: oftentimes we pass these under construction boards for what seems like an age and then one day we are confronted with a shiny new build – construction is complete.

DECIDING ON A STRUCTURE/YOUR POWERS –
ACTIVITY / KEY POINTS:

What is your group's short-term vision?

_____

_____

_____

_____

What is your organisation's longer-term vision?

_____

_____

_____

_____

_____

Are you aiming for growth?

_____

_____

_____

_____

_____

Does your vision include employing people, acquiring assets?

_____

_____

_____

_____

_____

Is your group to be run as a business, not for profit or a charity? (Note that not for profit and social enterprise ventures do not automatically qualify as charitable)

_____

_____

_____

_____

_____

How will you decide on a structure and who will be part of this decision?

_____

_____

_____

_____

_____

Why is this the best structure to achieve your aims/fulfil your vision?

_____

_____

_____

_____

_____

Comments:

_____

_____

_____

_____

The following may prove useful as a 'snapshot' to the level of work involved in progressing your vision into reality.

OVERVIEW: EXAMPLES OF REGISTRATION

Type of structure	Unconstituted group (unincorporated)	Constituted group (unincorporated)	Registered company	Charitable Incorporated Organisation (CIO)	Community Interest company (CIC)
Basics	1. Name of group	1. Name of group	1. Name of company 2. Address for Registered office	1. Name of charity 2. Address for Registered office	1. Name of CIC 2. Address for Registered office
People	Any number of people	Any number of people	Minimum of 1 person	Minimum of 3 people	Minimum of 1-3 people
Formal roles	None	Management board	1. Director 2. Shareholder 3. Person with Significant Control	Trustees	1. Director/s 2. Shareholder 3. Person with Significant Control
Documents	None	Constitution	1. Company Registration Form 2. Articles of Association 3. Memorandum	1. Constitution 2. Application (online) 3. Trustee declaration form	1. Company Registration form 2. Articles of Association 3. Memorandum 4. Application form to CIC Regulator
Specific	None	None	SIC Code – Standard industrial classification of economic activities	Objects	1. SIC Code – Standard industrial classification of economic activities 2. Asset Lock Nominee
Costs Optional?	None	None	Registration Fees - legal fees?	None -legal fees?	Registration Fees - legal fees?
Other	None	None	None	£5,000 annual income Copy of bank statement	None
Timing	No time constraints	2-4 weeks	1-3 months	3-6 months	1 -3 months

COMPLETING REGISTRATION – ACTIVITY/KEY STEPS:

What KEY steps do we need to take to complete registration?

1. _____

_____

_____

_____

2. _____

_____

_____

_____

3. _____

_____

_____

_____

_____

4. _____

_____

_____

_____

_____

5. _____

_____

_____

_____

_____

6. _____

_____

_____

_____

_____

_____

7. _____

_____

_____

_____

_____

Comments:

_____

_____

_____

_____

_____

_____

_____

_____

III. YOUR PEOPLE

Leading the way

An important part of laying the foundations includes identifying any leadership roles within the organisation. There are two key leadership roles that should feature:

- **Strategic** – This role takes a wider overview in the vision and direction of the organisation and how best it can be achieved
- **Operational** – This role is primarily responsible for putting this vision and direction into practice.

Whilst these roles may appear duplicating, they are not. What is often the case is that one person often duplicates themselves in the dual roles as opposed to having two separate people perform the distinction. Roles should, where possible, not be tied to a particular person; this point is crucial in regards to sustainability.

Does your organisation heavily rely on a person rather than a role?

If this is the case then you will run into problems if that particular person is no longer able to fulfil that role, and as has often happened in the past, the organisation ceases to exist.

A firm governance structure is something that will facilitate growth and seek to attract sustainable operational methods that will serve to ensure the group thrives and adapts to changes and, most importantly, survives.

LEADERSHIP AND OTHER ROLES

Leadership is a funny term; it can imply that somebody is in charge and this somebody has all the answers to in turn cascade to the non-leaders. I prefer to view leadership as a role that is not necessarily of higher importance. Rather it is a role that is required to ensure cohesion, motivation and goodwill amongst the team. An effective leader must be able to serve, have people skills and know how best to motivate the people he/she leads. Effective leaders often lead by example which means that no task should be considered of lesser importance. What is essential is that the leader of an organisation is able to see the bigger picture, something which a junior member of the team might not yet have grasped. However, the next important step is the ability to present the bigger picture to all members of the team in a way that can be digested and assimilated into practice. It is a good and effective leader who shares the load and ensures that the load is evenly distributed and delivered in a manner that serves the clear aims and purpose of the organisation.

ME, MYSELF AND I

Schools, community groups & statutory councils

My interest and experience in governance began about 15 years ago when I became a teacher governor at the request of my head teacher. School governor is one of those terms we hear all the time yet know very little about what the role entails. It is essentially a strategic position where one acts as a 'critical friend' to the senior leadership team of the school. Being prepared to read papers and reports, attend regular meetings and ask any difficult questions is integral to the role. I lasted about a year in that role as a school governor before I left primary teaching to become a full-time mum to my, then, two young children. However, my governing days were not left behind as I went on to become a community governor at my children's nursery before becoming a Chair of Governors at their primary school.

With my interest in governance ignited, I soon became involved with a neighbourhood forum in my local area. This was the precursor for a local campaign involving about 40 residents to set up a parish council. I chaired this campaign and went on to become the founding Chairman of the parish council for the first two years. This is London's first parish council and our small corner of North Westminster has indeed made history.

The parish council model is made up of varying numbers of local councillors and prioritises the need for paid staff to service the council. This is possible due to the fact that the parish council is able to charge a precept: a small tax to all local people, and for this reason it is a public body with full financial controls and is required to adhere to associated regulations. In many ways, it provides a system where local people can really do for self and it serves as the lowest tier of democracy here in the UK

Running concurrently to this wider community activity, just over 5 years ago, I was a succeeding co-founder of a small voluntary group called *Tell It Parents Action Group*. Forming this group was a natural response and development to a national campaign that aimed to address the disproportionately high numbers of black children leaving secondary school with little or no GCSE's, particularly English & Maths grades A-C. Local people were keen to have a dedicated service for parents in the local area, hence *Tell It Parents* Action Group was born. My co-founder has since left in favour of full time paid work and I have, in the main, carried on the group's work more or less single-handedly.

We operated as a fully constituted but unincorporated organisation with a small management team and our own two-signatory bank account. A natural progression has seen us register as a charitable interest organisation in recent months as a means of sustaining our growth and capacity to meet the growing need for increased parental support and a range of social and economic issues.

My experience of the two very different groups is relevant for the purpose of this guide.

Prior to CIO registration, *Tell It Parents* had the autonomy and freedom to conduct its business pretty much as it saw fit. It had clear aims and reviewed its objectives regularly to ensure its activities were in line with what users want or need. The biggest drawback was that it relied solely on the input of an individual to keep going and it is both my experience and belief that the days of the lone ranger are severely limited, if not over.

On the other hand, the parish council is set up in a way that it requires the input of many to keep business ticking over. There are a number of key roles to fulfil and each role is considered an integral part of the whole operation. In the event a councillor or indeed councillors are missing in action, it can sustain itself and replace those people if need be. Meetings are planned in advance and so long as numbers are quorate, meetings will and do go ahead.

I talk from such personal experience when I say it is a huge challenge to lead alone. Arguably, what is being led if one is 'leading' in isolation? I know without a doubt that a number of great ideas for community action are the seeds of individuals. Furthermore, a number of those individuals will testify that if they had waited for a team to emerge they would still be waiting. But I sense a changing climate where a growing number of people absolutely embrace the need for collective responsibility and the days of soldiering on alone are indeed numbered.

Working through these important steps presented here and laying the foundations will identify the various key roles and these roles will depend upon the governance structure your organisation chooses to adopt.

BENEFITS OF A STRATEGIC MANAGEMENT OR SOUNDING BOARD

The strategic component of any organisation is one which has the power to create, set and amend if necessary the mission and vision for the organisation. It further ensures that every decision made by the board is aimed at helping the organisation to realise its aims as identified in the mission statement.

An effective board is one which ensures

- The organisation's programmes and services are fit for purpose
- Policies governing all aspects of the operation are current, relevant and useful to all in achieving the aims of the organisation
- Financial procedures that are fit for purpose include budgets and monitoring spend. Such procedures also ensure that all other safeguarding matters are in place including insurance and any risk management
- Fundraising is a core component of the operation to ensure adequate resources are available to carry out its mission
- The role of the staff complements the role of board – there is no undermining
- Comprehensive and fair staff policy is implemented with a special relationship between the Board and the lead member of staff (CEO, Project manager etc.)
- Systems are in place for effective reporting, monitoring and maintaining an appropriate operational framework
- The reputation of the organisation is sound to include the behaviour of all board members and staff

Key roles for any organisation can include:

Strategic:	Operational:
Management Board	Director
Board of Directors	Project Leader
Trustees	Manager
Chair, Treasurer, Secretary,	Chief Executive Officer (CEO)
(all will be a part of any of the above boards)	Paid staff: Full time/Part time
Volunteers	Volunteers

There are no shortcuts to getting the 'right' people to form part of any management board as Directors or Trustees. This is a task that may prove time consuming as the most appropriate people are sourced to fill the positions.

It is helpful and useful to try and attract people who share the vision of your organisation (clear aims & objectives), maybe people who are already involved with your work would be prepared to step up and take on a leading role?

Or you may prefer to look for people with certain areas of expertise: for example, finance, fundraising, and communications, including online marketing and social media, are always key skills to bring to the table.

It is worth noting that even if your group opts not to pursue a formal registration route, it can be of huge value to have a group of people that can be called upon from time to time as a 'sounding' board. Airing your vison, aims and objectives to others with your best interests at heart is a good, informal way to review your practice to ensure that you are operating as effectively as you can.

The following exercises are useful in highlighting if there are any gaps in your organisation and what steps you can take to make your board fit for purpose.

YOUR PEOPLE – ACTIVITY/KEY POINTS:

Name the key people currently active in your group/organisation

_____

_____

_____

_____

Who are the thinkers?

_____

_____

_____

_____

Who are the doers?

_____

_____

_____

_____

What are the key roles needed in order to deliver your aims/objectives?
Strategic:

_____

_____

_____

_____

_____

_____

Operational:

_____

_____

_____

_____

How many people do you have who are willing to act as Trustees, volunteers etc.?

_____

_____

_____

_____

How will you go about recruiting more people?

_____

_____

_____

_____

Comments:

_____

_____

_____

_____

_____

_____

_____

OTHER USEFUL CONSIDERATIONS

In addition to the purpose, powers and people sections of your governance structure, it is helpful to set out from the onset some of the following:

i. Time commitments

In order for the process to run as smoothly as possible, it is important to outline the estimated time commitment for key people in the group. It is essential for those who take on a leading role to know in advance what level of input is required to carry out their duties. Having a calendar of dates scheduled year on year is an effective way of making sure other commitments do not interfere with group meetings. There is nothing worse than absenteeism on a regular basis. Missing persons at meetings often leads to a stalling of progress and having to revisit items discussed to bring everyone up to speed. Naturally, there will be times when nonattendance at a meeting happens and groups will need to think carefully about how any key decisions made at meetings will be recorded and communicated.

Of note is the fact that in order for meetings to be useful and productive, some work has to be done in between meetings with regards to setting agendas, typing up minutes, reading any prepared papers in advance of meetings (that includes minutes of the previous meeting) and sending any associated internal communications. All of these things must be considered when calculating the time commitment that a key member is expected to set aside for their duties.

ii. All or Nothing

When first starting out, most groups prefer to conduct all business via the whole group. This is useful in the first 6-12 months of operation to ensure that all involved have a say in setting up and getting the process started. After the first few months, depending on the size and number of key members, your group may opt to use a scheme of delegation. This enables certain activities to be passed down to a smaller group of people which may be referred to as a committee or a working group, and facilitates greater autonomy in getting things done, especially if there is more than one project issue being addressed.

This smaller group will have greater flexibility to meet and progress projects or issues. A decision to operate in this manner can form part of your governance documents which should clearly state how you will carry out your aims as well as how you intend to get things done.

iii. Code of conduct

This is an additional tool that should help to keep meetings on task and provide a point of reference if and when somebody strays from the appropriate behaviour desirable at meetings.

It can refer to things such as:
- Attending all meetings as required
- Sending apologies if unable to attend
- How opinions/points of view will be sought and heard during meetings
- The need to treat everyone respectfully
- **See part 2b**

To conclude...

- Agendas should be linked to specific points in the organisations operations or business plan to ensure key issues are being dealt with.
- Meetings should be productive and conducted with a level of efficiency.
- Needs of board members, staff and volunteers should be identified and where possible funding sought to provide training that equips individuals with the skills and knowledge to do the tasks in hand.
- Bringing in expertise should be considered to continuously reflect on developing the organisation's effectiveness.

Notice how once the new build is in place and working smoothly, there is an assumption that the foundations are doing their job and it is only if/when problems arise that these foundations may come under close inspection. They are not to be ignored, rather they should be constantly acknowledged as working properly or the whole thing will fall flat.

Above all, the foundations are not in any way intended to detract from the important day to day work of the group. They shouldn't be seen as a set of bureaucratic extras, instead they are a solid set of working principles upon which the work of the group is carried out.

OTHER USEFUL CONSIDERATIONS – ACTIVITY/KEY POINTS:

How often will the meetings take place (6-8 weeks is an average timing)

_____

_____

_____

_____

_____

How long will each meeting last?

_____

_____

_____

_____

Who will be responsible for communicating dates of meetings?

_____

_____

_____

_____

Who will set the agenda?

_____

_____

_____

_____

Who will take minutes, type up & circulate?

_____

_____

___

How many meetings can a person miss before any action is taken?

___

___

___

___

Can anything be done to encourage/reward regular attendance/input?

___

___

___

___

Will all meetings be full group meetings?

___

___

___

___

Will there be smaller committees or working groups – why?

___

___

___

___

___

How will this be decided?

_____
_____
_____
_____
_____
_____

What might be some useful committees or working groups?

_____
_____
_____
_____
_____
_____

Comments:

_____
_____
_____
_____
_____
_____
_____

Part 2 b.
Laying Foundations with Love

The eye never forgets what the heart has seen

African proverb

THE CALL TO LOVE

Many governance documents include a section that outlines an expected Code of Conduct. This section is geared towards that. However, instead of simply listing a set of expected behaviours, I feel it is necessary to provide more depth to this aspect of the process.

In part one of this guide, I make reference to the fact that certain historic practices have impacted on our ability to work together productively. For example, the affiliation many of us have with the various Caribbean Islands often reinforces the separation as many of us cling tightly to the differences between the islands in favour of embracing the range of different flags as opposed to embracing the many commonalities. This serves to render us separate from each other. Equally, there is a large and growing number of black empowerment programmes to choose from that are all intended as forms of edification to heal the malaise endemic in our community. Finding the most appropriate programmes to fit our needs can at times prove both overwhelming and challenging.

In view of the fact that our natural way of being as African people, living in Ubuntu based humanity, with a real sense of community, was so brutally interrupted, many would be hard pressed not to acknowledge that we are yet to return to our natural state. Examples abound of the lack of love and regard we have for those who share our image. We must all be familiar with a common story of an encounter with a black owned business or event where things didn't run smoothly or go to plan and the well-used rhetoric here often being "I won't be going back there". I once saw a social media post which stated: *"If you are not happy with the service you have received today, tell me so I can put it right"*. This is an act of love and something very few of us can do both sincerely and routinely.

The ongoing lack of a widely accepted common culture and an absence of traditional practices, have created a fragile foundation upon which to build a strong sense of identity. Can a people with no real common consensus of what constitutes our culture or traditions agree on a best way forward?

I am not suggesting that we do away with the many forward-thinking programmes or that these tools and methods be abandoned. What I am suggesting is that there is something we all need without question and that something is love. This section is all about the Call to Love.

For the final part of this guide, it's worth remembering that the only thing that really matters in life is LOVE, so this final section is all about strengthening our individual and collective capacities to give and receive love.

In 2002, I developed a course for women called *A Call to Love*. This six week course was aimed at creating a safe space for women of African heritage to explore our experiences via a historical and experiential lens in order to make sense of how we arrived, individually, at our understanding of giving, receiving and sharing love. A lasting legacy of this course is the Loving Principles, a set of 12 qualities that, together, when practised and emitted on a regular basis have the transformational effect of us *being* in love; to facilitate a more loving approach to relating to self and others. The course was experiential in nature and a number of women who took the course continue to practice these principles and incorporate them into their daily lives, present day.

WHY THE 12 LOVING PRINCIPLES?

Love is not something that we can give or get per se, it is more something that we are being, it is at the core of our very existence and some may argue that this is our sole purpose on earth: to be love!

Ask anybody "what is love?" and you are likely to be met with a plethora of suggestions ranging from a feeling of butterflies in the stomach to a warm, giddy feeling triggered by a significant other. Numerous people have also referred to there being different types of love and many believe that the love one holds for a child differs from the love of a romantic union.

Love is love is love, albeit expressed in different ways: the way we show our children love, differs from the love that we may have for a friend and ultimately the love expressed within the confines of a romantic union includes the connecting of hearts and minds and the sacred act of sharing our bodies physically, emotionally and spiritually. And whilst some of us believe that love is a feeling, the Loving Principles go further in suggesting that love is something we are: a way of being and doing that includes our attitude, our personal qualities and the very way we go about our daily interactions with ourselves and the world.

It is hard to recognise, feel and accept love if we are not being loving and there is a need to give in order to receive. For love to live in our hearts, we need to be capable of gratitude, to be open to what we are able to give and receive on a daily basis no matter how seemingly small.

LOVE IS THE ANTIDOTE TO PAIN

It has long been accepted that due to the historic legacy of the insubordination of our people at the hands of cruel, inhumane practices on all levels. On a physical, emotional, mental and spiritual level, we are in need of self-healing. Not to distract from the positive energy of theses ensuing pages, it must be noted that a mirage of malaise is endemic present day. This is witnessed by prevailing beliefs centred on the lack of adequate unity amongst us and the lack of support for our own, emotionally, economically and otherwise.

I myself have witnessed warring factions within groups of supposedly positive and 'forward-thinking' people, and don't even get me started on the different groups that on the surface have similar aims. People have been referred to as snakes, liars and false prophets. And this amongst the 'conscious and awakened' section of the community!

SO, WHAT ARE THE LOVING PRINCIPLES?

The Loving Principles are a set of 12 loving qualities of being and doing:

1. **Acceptance**
2. **Commitment**
3. **Compassion**
4. **Faith**
5. **Forgiveness**
6. **Non-Judgement**
7. **Patience**

8. **Release**
9. **Respect**
10. **Trust**
11. **Truth**
12. **Selflessness**

On the surface, I am sure we are all too familiar with every single one of these qualities. The challenge is to embrace these at a deeper level, on a daily basis and to apply them to our everyday interactions. Let's take a look at each one briefly in turn.

Acceptance: This is so important for us all. Often, we are quick to see the things in ourselves and others that we don't like. Accepting them diffuses the power such things may have over us and is a first step to actioning change whether that is doing something about the very thing that irks us or knowing that there is nothing that can be done. It is only when we truly are working on accepting ourselves in our entirety that we are able to extend this to the acceptance of others.

Example: Accepting that we have different experiences, viewpoints and ways of going about things is a key stage to reaching a compromise which always has a role in any organisation or group activity.

Commitment: This is the long game. Rarely does something meaningful happen overnight. Therefore, in order to achieve the best results possible under any circumstances, requires the long haul. Too often some of us bail out at the first sign of difficulty. This could be concerning any number of things ranging from studies, home, work and business goals, to personal relationships and learning new skills.

Commitment is recognising that there will be times we are challenged, tired or simply fed up. Do we give up? No. This is not about ploughing on with ways that are ineffective, rather if we are committed to achieving something, we are open to changing tack where necessary to keep a focus on the end goal.

Example: Anybody serious about playing an integral role in any group or organisation needs to be committed; they need to be able to sustain their involvement over a period of time. This is the long game.

Compassion: Look up the definition of *compassion* and there are a number of words that can be used in its place: *empathy, care, understanding, concern* and *kindness* to name a few. In this cut-throat climate of every man for himself, compassion is a much-needed principle that seeks to acknowledge that humanity experiences suffering on all levels and often we have no details of the path trodden by another. I take from this the simple need to be kind. Kindness is a truly underrated act of love, however; it is often the foundation for leaving another with a feeling of warmth. Irrespective of what we say or do, it's often how we make a person feel that has lasting benefits.

Example: Being able to alter one's perspective to include the perspective of another is crucial in any group or organisation that has set itself up to help others. Start at home and apply this principle within your group/organisation.

Faith: Ask yourself what you place your faith in. Do you believe that things will always go wrong or do you believe that you are deserving of positivity? Wherever we place our faith is likely what we will see show up for ourselves. The old observation of seeing the glass half full or half empty is valid here. Some people believe in struggle and therefore this is what they will create. None of us like to be proved wrong, so even if the outcome is to our detriment, the fact that we 'always knew' something wasn't going to work out or was too good to be true provides some comfort to the all-knowing ego.

Ultimately, faith on a spiritual level, requires us to believe in something we cannot see. However, placing blind faith in any belief system without applying positive faith in ourselves doesn't work.

Example: Do you believe the group will fail or succeed? What is your ongoing narrative about any pitfalls you may encounter? Will you revert to the worn out belief that there is just a lack of support? Or do you truly believe your venture will be supported somehow?

Forgiveness: Forgiveness generally generates the most conversation as it is one of the most challenging principles to practise. The saying goes 'you can forgive but you mustn't forget'. Actually, you must forget any associated pain in order to complete forgiveness. By banking the pain caused by the unforgiving act, it remains accessible to the subconscious mind and can be triggered to surface if anything resembling that act were to reoccur. This is why the principle of release is an integral part of being and doing in love.

Example: Maybe this is the latest in a long line of attempts to get organised. Have you harboured ill feeling from past failures or experiences with previous groups or organisations? Let that baggage go. Don't apply the characteristics of past failed projects to your new project. Go into it with a clean slate.

Non-Judgement: This often goes hand in hand with acceptance simply because the things we pass judgement on tend to be less favourable to our expectations, standards or liking. Watching another and passing a judgement based on the shallowness of looks is something we do most likely if we have issues with our own physical appearance. Putting in our two pennies worth on hearing of another's personal plight is short sighted and indicative of the harsh judgment we likely meter out to ourselves. The saying 'don't judge another until you've walked a mile in their shoes' is something we need to remember daily not just for others but also for ourselves. We are often our own worst judge and jury.

Example: To what extent can you set aside your personal views and opinions when working with others? Are those who don't hold the same views as you wrong? It's important to validate the ideas and strengths of others by simply acknowledging them. Listen and 'hear' what others are trying to convey in the same way you want your own ideas and strengths to be validated and 'heard' by others.

Patience: So how long should we wait for something or someone? How long is a piece of string? I like to partner this principle with *commitment*. It will take as long as it takes. This is not about apathy, it is about knowing that obstacles are sometimes sent to test our resolve. Overcoming adversity requires not only a committed stance but the courage to withstand the first hurdle and the patience to continue in the face of ongoing challenges.

Example: Do you accept that it's taken centuries for this state of malaise to become embedded globally and thus it will take a long, sustained effort to effect lasting change? Getting organised is but a first step in the long process.

Release: Release is part of forgiveness. Forgiveness is not entirely possible without release. When asked how we release, we should understand that some form of physical ritual most likely needs to accompany any thought process of letting go of unwanted feelings and past hurts. Yes, we can think of letting go, but it's also useful to do something physical that is symbolic of getting the pain out of ourselves. Writing, exercise, visualisation, and deep breathing can all assist with this process of truly letting go of painful thoughts and feelings that no longer serve us. And this is a key point: those feelings served us in the moment we were hurt; the moment we allowed someone to hurt us. If you're feelings are unresolved, resolve them by viewing the past as a stepping stone. Perhaps it needed to happen to open your eyes to something new or some pattern of behaviour you were then expressing.

Example: Are you prepared to rewrite the narratives of the past and drop any focus on failures of black groups and organisations? Are you willing to understand that everyone in your life showed up for a purpose? In fact, it's entirely possible that the people who are showing up to be part of your new project are showing up for a reason that aligns with the universe's plan for it, reasons we cannot always see coming. If you begin with yourself, you will be better equipped to direct the group and hold it together in the face of obstacles, challenges, and any adversity that may occur among members.

Respect: Now this a funny one. We hear this word bandied around all day long in certain circles and it is often quoted that respect is something that needs to be earned; it is not an automatic right. This focus is on the receiving end. What about the giving end? Is the giving of respect conditional upon receiving it? If so who gives first? You see the nonsense here. This is perhaps one of the most misunderstood principles that would make life a lot easier if we truly practised what we preached.

Example: Can you treat others with respect at all times in the absence of mutual agreement? Can you let others know in a respectful manner that their views differ from yours in your effort to work together?

Trust: Trust is perhaps one of the most fragile principles as it can be wiped out at the drop of a hat. It's often based on our gut instinct about people, but as we work with others, we learn by their actions whether or not we should continue that trust. Each of us must be doing the best we can at any given time so that we ourselves are deemed trustworthy. The challenge is to maintain the trust you have built for yourself and this will translate into the trust you are able to extend to others. Without trust, there is little hope.

Example: Are you trustworthy? How can you demonstrate and model trust to others in a group situation? How do you determine if someone is trustworthy?

Truth: How many of us live our truth every moment of every day? Does the company we keep define the level of truth we are able to emit? Do we look for sincere ways of communicating our truth regardless of another's position? To live from a position of truth we need the company of some of the other principles such as acceptance and trust. We need to know who we are and what matters to us regardless of whether this differs from another.

Example: Can you communicate honestly in an open forum? Have you honestly identified your personal reasons for being involved in any group or organisation?

Selflessness: Coupled with compassion this is a truly heavyweight act of love. Going back to respect, how many of us are able to act unconditionally, not expecting anything in return when we give of ourselves? Maybe we can last for a week, a month or a year, and then we sit back and list all the things we have done and seek to balance this against the return. 'Investing' in another is not selfless if we are waiting for a return. Selflessness requires that we act purely out of love and concern and the only 'payback' is the knowledge that we have been of service. For many people, this is a tough one because our ego requires that we pay attention to self not selflessness.

Example: Are you expecting some return for your involvement in any group setting? Would you be content to take on any role that is important for the group's success whether it's leading, administrative work, volunteering, setting up for events, or even helping to clean up after an event?

LOVE IS A SPIRITUAL THING

For some, the inclusion of the preceding section may appear questionable. This is likely the case for those of us who have become entrenched in a Western way of working. We may have witnessed some cut-throat behaviours and forced smiles in the name of professionalism and climbing the career ladder. Mimicking behaviours that are not in line with our natural state of being is a recipe for disaster and only serves to reinforce the 'popular' belief that we cannot do and achieve for ourselves as a people.

Arguably, if any attempts for betterment are not guided by love, the challenge will persist. This guide can in no way do justice to the many spiritual practices that serve to support the increase of joy and the decrease of sorrow in the black community, but it's a start. Oftentimes, mention is made about the success of other communities, in particular the Asian community. Accepting they too are not one homogenous group, there are some common practices I have noted on several occasions. If ever you have been one of the first customers at your local Asian owned corner shop, you may have caught a whiff of the incense they burn as part of a morning ritual. Having patronised an Asian-owned nail shop, I have seen their altar take pride of place in the reception area. Where are our supporting practices and rituals in our efforts to come together, work together and stay together to address the many ills?

There are many rituals we must embrace to support the release of love in our community, but we must begin with ourselves and apply the Loving principles coupled with an intellectual appreciation. Spiritual practices will provide more depth and we need to go deeper.

THE LOVING PRINCIPLES – ACTIVITY/KEY POINTS:

1) Think of examples when each principle has a role to play in the day to day management/operations of your group/organisation.

2) Think also about the consequences in the absence of that principle in any given example.

Acceptance: _____

_____

_____

Commitment: _____

_____

_____

Compassion: _____

_____

_____

Faith: _____

_____

_____

Forgiveness: _____

_____

_____

Non-judgement: _____

_____

_____

_____

_____

Patience: _____

_____

_____

Release: _____

_____

_____

Respect: _____

_____

_____

Trust: _____

_____

_____

Truth: _____

_____

_____

Selflessness: _____

_____

_____

Comments: _____

_____

_____

_____

_____

_____

END NOTE

There is a lot to be said for being a well thought through and tightly organised force to be reckoned with. A group or organisation that has clear aims and clearly identified operating procedures for how these aims will be achieved, is on the road to fulfilling a lasting vison.

This guide is not intended to dictate which structure is the most suited to your group; it is not intended to dictate one particular route, rather the overview and exercises herein aim to provide a framework by which you can arrive at this conclusion yourself as a collective body responsible for birthing or developing the organisation of your vision. It is hoped that having digested the contents, many will accept that operating without a lack of structure, an agreed process of delivery and a road map for the journey forwards is like trying to cook with no recipe and no fuel!

The exercises offered should be accepted and viewed as an integral part of the process of getting organised and will provide a useful framework for team building, sharing ideas and developing effective working relations. If used as a starting point or as a means to review current practice, such exercises provide an opportunity to flush out any poor practices, underlying tensions or disagreements. This is all part of the process and, if applied in the correct manner, any dwelling on such matters will be minimised by integrating the Loving principles as part of the journey forward.

The systematic barriers designed to maintain the status quo regarding the widely documented disadvantage and malaise that continues to plague our communities, are unlikely to be dismantled by those who reap the benefits of this inequality and advantage. In fact, it is foolhardy to expect those responsible for establishing such systems to freely and willingly let go of that which serves their best interests.

Thus, we, as active members of the black community, need to take ownership of advancing our own cause, bettering ourselves, our families and our communities in a way that keeps the wheels of change in motion. For this we need to recognise the inherent value in organising ourselves and sustaining that high level of organisation as a means of realising and actualising the depth of our potential.

We, We, We.

I sincerely hope I have laid out some weighty considerations, many of which have impacted us from our past, some clear routes for how we can mobilise presently and of course the love that we need to harness and stockpile going forward.

Let's get organised and let's make love an integral part of our works.

APPENDIX

EXAMPLE MODELS OF STRUCTURES

Business model
i.e. Company, Charity or Community Interest Organisation (CIO)

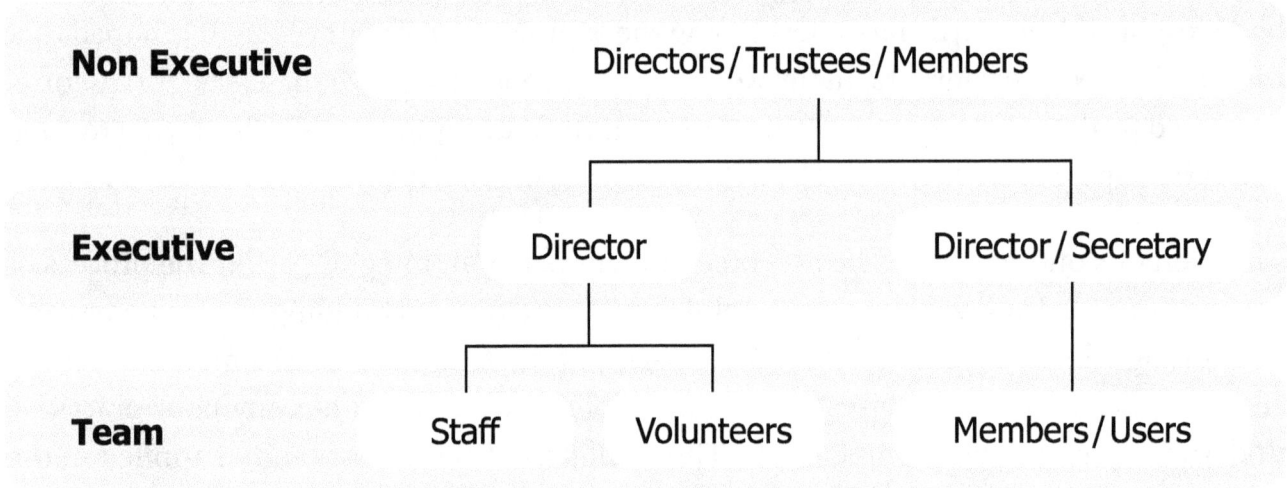

Non Executive	Directors/Trustees/Members	
Executive	Director	Director/Secretary
Team	Staff Volunteers	Members/Users

Community Organisation model
i.e., Community Interest Company (CIC)
or Unincorporated association (Community Group)

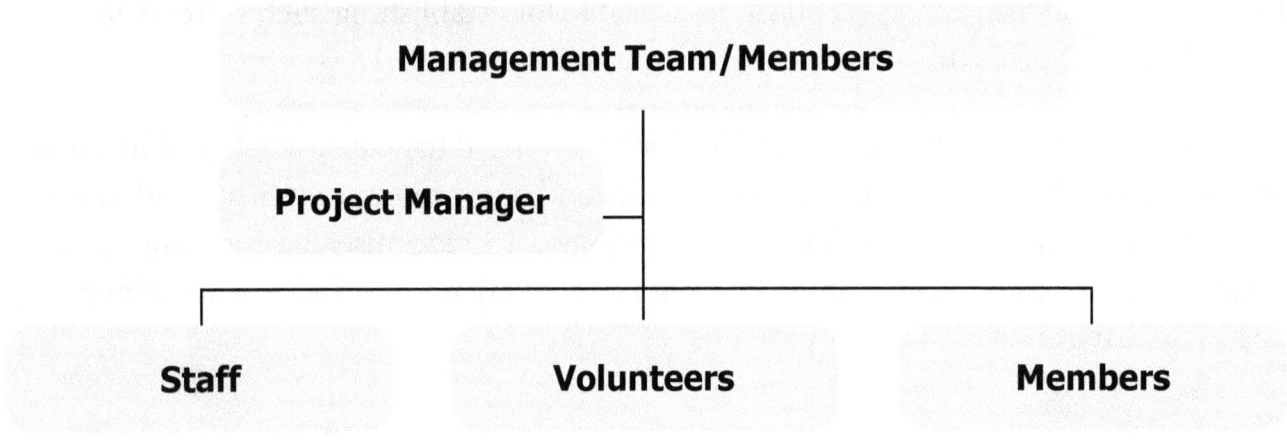

Management Team/Members

Project Manager

Staff   **Volunteers**   **Members**

EXAMPLE DECISION MAKING PROCESS/STRUCTURES

Type of structure	Advantages/Pros	Disadvantages/Cons
No structure	Free of rules & bureaucracy Sounds nice & organic	Can breed chaos Can breed hidden agendas & factions
Majority Rule	Fair voting system Many aware of process Can be time friendly	Can cause divisions; winners & losers Hard to get 'losers' to commit to decision of 'winners'
Hierarchy	Clear line of accountability & responsibility Clear structure	Not representative of all Not all views heard or taken into account Do as I say mentality
Consensual	Ideal for exploring all views Mutuality is the end game Decisions well thought out Encourages cooperation & input at all levels	Time consuming Can be frustrating Loving Principles must be fully embraced as part of the process e.g. good listening skills, respect, patience, etc. all required
Unanimity	Everyone in complete agreement!	Rarely occurs Nigh impossible to achieve with more than 2 people

FURTHER SUGGESTED RESEARCH & READING

Further information on the various Governance structures are often available from your local Voluntary Action (VA) organisation. Most areas have a VA organisation that provides a range of services for local non-profit community groups and charities.

The following websites are integral to the registration process:

For further information on company registration:

www.gov.uk/government/organisations/companies-house

For further information on CIC registration:

www.gov.uk/government/organisations/office-of-the-regulator-of-community-interest-companies

For further information on charity registration:

www.gov.uk/government/organisations/charity-commission

For further information on registration with HMRC:

www.gov.uk/charity-recognition-hmrc

USEFUL BOOK LIST

1. **Adofo, Dalian**: Ancestral Voices – Spirit is Eternal, 2016
2. **Ani, Marimba**: Yurunga: An African centred Critique of European Cultural Thought & Behaviour, 1994
3. **Cress Welsing, Frances**: The Isis Papers: The Code to the Colours, 1991
4. **DeGruy Joy Angela**: Post Traumatic Slave Syndrome: America's legacy of Enduring Injury & Healing, 2005
5. **Kunjufu, Jawanza**: Black Economics: Solutions for Economic & Community Empowerment, 2002
6. **Walker, Robin**: When We Ruled: The Ancient & Mediaeval History of Black Civilisations, 2011
7. **Wills, Jane**: Locating Localism: Statecraft, citizenship & democracy, 2016

www.ingramcontent.com/pod-product-compliance
Lightning Source LLC
Chambersburg PA
CBHW061105210326
41597CB00021B/3985